$7.95 le

of the

Alamo

by

Ben H. Procter

Texas State Historical Association

Library of Congress Catalog Card Number: 86-050749

ISBN 0-87611-081-2 Paperback edition

At San Antonio on December 4, 1835, a leathery-faced frontiersman named Ben Milam emerged from the tent of General Edward Burleson who commanded a motley group of Texans euphemistically called an army. He was not happy. During the past few hours word had arrived that the Mexican forces in the city, under General Martín Perfecto de Cós, were "in a state of confusion" and that their military strength had been grossly exaggerated. Yet Burleson, despite Milam's urgent pleas to storm the enemy defenses, had decided to withdraw; after all, the Texans had neither the discipline nor training to defeat army regulars who were strongly fortified and well concealed. But Milam believed that such inaction would mean the "breaking up of the volunteer army, which was the last hope of Texas." So to his countrymen he voiced his discontent—and concern—then dramatically drew a line across the ground as a challenge for brave men to respond, and yelled:

"Who will follow Old Ben Milam?"

Immediately shouts of approval rang out, and some three hundred fellow soldiers stepped forward to the order of "fall in line." In a test of wills against a superior officer Milam had won.

For the next few days the Texans furiously attacked the enemy in their own unique manner. Although dividing into two separate forces, they followed identical assault patterns. From street to rooftop, from fence to house, they battled the Mexican defenders, applying frontier techniques of fighting with telling effect. Their small arms fire was devastating, their relentless advance demoralizing. Even when Cós withdrew across the San Antonio River to a new line of defense at the mission San Antonio de Valero (better known as the Alamo) and after Mexican reinforcements arrived on December 8, the situation remained relatively unchanged; Cós realized that his army was facing annihilation by these fiercely attacking rebels. Early the next morning he offered terms of surrender, promising to leave Texas forever. Texans had at last driven the Mexican military from their land.

The capture of San Antonio crowned Texas efforts of the previous two months. Late in September, 1835, Cós had dispatched Lieutenant Francisco Castaneda with a company of 180 men to confiscate an iron cannon which the army had given to the citizens of Gonazles for protection against marauding Indians. But on October 2 the Texans had reacted defiantly against such action. They had insolently placed a flag on the six-pounder with the words "COME AND TAKE IT" and then had proceeded to initiate the Lexington and Concord of the Texas Revolution; they had attacked and routed the Mexican force. A week later forty Texans had captured Goliad, including all military stores at the mission of La Bahía. And while men were rushing toward San Antonio to besiege Cós and Colonel Domingo de Ugartechea, an ad hoc state government—ironically called the Permanent Council—was meeting at San Felipe de Austin. Besides appointing Stephen F. Austin to command the "Army of the People," which was assembling near San Antonio, and sending him more men and supplies, the Council established a postal system, commissioned privateers to attack ships of the Mexican merchant marine, and instructed Thomas F. McKinney to negotiate a $100,000 loan from the United States. But most important it took steps to inform Americans everywhere about what was happening in Texas.

So by November, 1835, the word was out; Texans were fighting in behalf of principles dear to the American heart—liberty and justice and, perhaps, independence. At Washington-on-the-Brazos on November 3, delegates from twelve municipalities and two departments replaced the Permanent Council with a stronger, more effective government, known as the General Consultation. Then, in words reminiscent of 1776, they reasserted their belief in the "natural rights" of man; their ardent conviction that an independent government should be established in the place of a tyrannous, outmoded one; their dogged determination to uphold the torch of

Alamo Church and Plaza, c. 1861. Courtesy Daughters of the Republic of Texas Library, San Antonio.

liberty; and, as Thomas Jefferson had put it in 1775, "to die as free men rather than live as slaves." To secure these ends they chose Branch T. Archer, William H. Wharton, and Stephen F. Austin as commissioners to the United States, their purpose specifically being to enlist recruits to fight for Texas and to acquire financial aid. The General Consultation even provided for another temporary government and elected Henry Smith of the newly formed Department of the Brazos as provisional governor. And to protect the state against Mexican vengeance, to uphold their decisions, and possibly to send a punitive expedition against Mexico, they appointed Sam Houston as commander-in-chief of a nonexistent regular army. Although adjourning on November 14, they set a meeting for March 1, at which time they would decide whether to renegotiate their status with Mexico or declare independence.

Such stirring events inspired many Americans to respond enthusiastically to the Texas cause. In New York and Boston huge throngs in mass meetings denounced Mexican oppression and pledged help to free Texas. In Philadelphia, a crowd burned the Mexican dictator Antonio López de Santa Anna in effigy. At Newport, Kentucky, the young industrialist Sidney Sherman sold his business to finance a company of fighting men, known as "The Buck Eye Rangers." In Tennessee, David Crockett, bitterly reflecting upon his defeat in the congressional elections by the Jackson forces, decided to build a new life elsewhere and told his constituents to "go to hell." With Texas lands as a lure and the promise of adventure seemingly assured, he enlisted a company of sharpshooters, soon to be called the "Tennessee Mounted Volunteers." At Natchitoches, Louisiana, attorney Daniel Cloud, responding to Sam Houston's appeal to "come with a good rifle and 100 rounds of ammunition —and come soon," gave up a promising law practice. And from the lower Mississippi River Valley came "Ringtail Roarers"—men who claimed to be half horse and half alligator—arrogant, muscle-proud men, magnificent fighters, insufferable braggarts and story-tellers of the Crockett mold, given to hyperbole and extensions of the truth. Proud of their

Portrait of David Crockett by William Henry Huddle. Courtesy Archives Division, Texas State Library.

country, they reveled in being called Americans; and they now recognized an opportunity to extend American mores and institutions to a less fortunate Mexican population, a chance to demonstrate their physical prowess while striking a blow in behalf of liberty. Against a tyrannical government, against a dictator demanding conformity and obedience, indeed against anyone who would challenge their rights, these men were ready to fight.

But soon after Cós's surrender at San Antonio in December, despite the activities and enthusiasm of such supporters, a disastrous trend seemed to be developing in Texas. The unity among Texans, so necessary for victory and survival, had disappeared. Some bickering possibly developed because the Texans thought that all danger had passed once Cós had left San Antonio for the Rio Grande. In fact, many volunteers from the Mississippi River Valley, confident in their own fighting ability, wanted to march south against Mexico itself. A more apparent reason for disunity, however, was a flaw in the constitutional makeup of the government which had failed to define clearly the powers of its different branches. Within a short time Governor Smith and the council were at odds, arguing over their assumed rights as well as over the prudence of certain policies. Eventually the council members tried to impeach Smith and he, refusing to accept their decision, tried, in turn, to dismiss them.

The Texas military reflected the weaknesses of such divided leadership. For instance, the council members adopted a plan for a campaign against Matamoros (just across the Rio Grande from present-day Brownsville), appointing on separate occasions Frank W. Johnson and James W. Fannin, Jr. to lead the operation. On the other hand Governor Smith ordered General Sam Houston, who was opposed to the Matamoros project, to take charge of the troops. Near Refugio all three commanders joined their army and attempted to take command. In a popular referendum—a common practice among volunteer troops—the army selected Fannin as its leader. Houston immediately voiced his disapproval of the expedition, placed himself on a leave of absence from the army until March 1 and left for East Texas to negotiate treaties of peace with the Cherokees.

But on January 17, 1836, before leaving Refugio, Houston ordered Colonel James Bowie with approximately thirty men to go to San Antonio, their specific purpose being to demolish the Alamo, abandon the city, and withdraw the Texas military forces to a more protected area around Gonzales. Bowie, as one historian put it, was no "messenger boy." At six feet one inch in height, 180 pounds, finely muscled and well proportioned for a man of forty, he was an imposing individual, surely much larger than most men of that era (before balanced nutrition affected size). Although his features were regular, his blue-gray eyes, deep-set and eerily penetrating, dominated a usually unsmiling, sunburned face, framed by chestnut brown, almost reddish, hair. And if his countenance was not impressive and foreboding to most men, surely his character and reputation were. Under a deceptively calm, often mild, demeanor existed a person who was lethal and completely blind to fear. Whenever a crisis had occurred in his life, he had always met and been equal to the challenge; he was, as J. Frank Dobie observed, "at home with bellowing alligators in the marshes, with mustangs and mustangers on the prairies, and with lawyers who 'would circumvent God'." His early escapades as a slaver with the pirate Jean Lafitte and as a filibusterer with Dr. James Long placed him in the realm of legend; his campaigns against the Indians as a colonel in the Texas Rangers during the early 1830s earned him the name of "the young lion" and enhanced this growing reputation; and his duels, using a huge knife bearing his name (a fearful-looking weapon), assured him not just of immediate awe and respect but of immortality.

Yet Jim Bowie had another side to him. Although a tough and uncompromising foe, he could be remarkably gentle. To women he was courtly and kind, to people in distress a Good Samaritan, to men under his command a father figure and concerned leader. Nor was he simply a rough-and-tumble adventurer; on the contrary he was fairly well educated for the time, speaking both French and Spanish almost fluently. And he moved about easily in a more sophisticated society, his manners refined and his speech surprisingly polished and smooth—only his blue-gray eyes could be storm signals alerting wary opponents of imminent danger. Without a doubt the blonde and beautiful Ursula María de Veramendi, the eldest daughter of vice governor of Coahuila and Texas Juan Martín de Veramendi and, at nineteen, the richest girl in San Antonio recognized a certain softness and gentleness about him. They were married in 1831, and their love was real, even though Bowie was absent much of the time on business trips. In September, 1833, when a cholera epidemic decimated his family in three days, taking the beautiful Ursula and their two infant children, as well as her mother and father, he was devastated. He lost interest for a time in business and in adventurous escapades, but uncharacteristically gave way to frequent bouts of drunkenness. Not until he became involved in other activities—fighting marauding Indians, engaging in land speculation, participating in the stirring events which were leading Texans into revolution—did his mourning become somewhat assuaged.

By January, 1836, however, Bowie had sufficiently recovered from personal grief to warrant command, evoking from Sam Houston the statement that "there is no man on whose forecast, prudence, and valor, I place a higher estimate." So on January 19 he rode into San Antonio and delivered his instructions to Colonel James C. Neill who had been left in charge of the area. Then the two men surveyed their surroundings and evaluated their situation. It was not encouraging. The mission San Antonio de Valero, founded in 1718 and better known as the Alamo because a presidial cavalry unit (the Flying Company of San José y Santiago del Alamos de Parras) occupied the area from 1801 to 1825, was in a state of disrepair and far too large to defend, at least with the present complement of Texans (Neill with eighty men and Bowie with thirty). Used as a military fort since 1801 but, as one of Bowie's men observed, "plainly" not "built by a military people for a fortress," it followed much the same pattern as the other four Franciscan missions which had been established along the San Antonio River. Approximately three acres in size, it had a large courtyard or plaza rectangularly shaped—154 yards long and 54 yards wide—bordered by stone walls which were three-to-four feet thick but only nine-to-twelve-feet high. On the north and west sides small adobe rooms and structures reinforced the walls, while on the south a long one-story building known as the "low barracks" added considerable support. In this area, also, a ten-foot wide passageway provided the main entrance into the courtyard. To the east a two-story mission convent, sometimes called the "long barracks" (approximately 200 feet in length), provided more than adequate protection, especially since the higher vantage point would allow defenders to survey uninterrupted the old convent plaza and mission corral just to the east. Yet obviously apparent was a gap or indenture on the southeastern side because the uniquely structured Alamo chapel, its rooms partly filled with debris from a caved-in roof, was fifty yards distant from the southeastern corner of the long barracks and could be considered only a partial hindrance to an attacking enemy. As a consequence, just prior to the assault by Ben Milam and the Texans in December, 1835, General Cós had constructed a low and ineffectual rampart of dirt and timber across the open space from the chapel to the barracks.

But even if the Alamo had had outstanding fortifications, Colonels Neill and Bowie would have had considerable difficulty in its defense. Besides having only 110 men—Bowie estimated that a force of 1,000 was needed—they had no money to buy military stores or pay the soldiers, no food or clothing (and only the promises from local citizens for aid), no adequate number of horses either for a scout or for transportation. As for military discipline among the troops, there was none. The men did as they pleased, sometimes refusing either to drill or go on patrol. Nor was Neill surprised at the increasing number of desertions since many of the men had only "one blanket and one shirt," and, as he wrote Governor Smith on January 6, "If there has ever been a dollar here I have no knowledge of it."

Despite such odds and despite Sam Houston's orders, Neill and Bowie were unwilling to abandon San Antonio and demolish the Alamo. Their reasons? Officially they stated that there was no transportation for the artillery. But their feelings ran much deeper. Actually they believed that the future of Texas depended upon keeping San Antonio out of enemy hands. Furthermore, the Alamo had an intangible, almost mystical effect upon the men, a definite transformation taking place once they were inside its walls. James Butler "Jim" Bonham, who had recently arrived from South Carolina and joined up with Bowie, had been a wanderer all his life; yet he found unbelievable solace and peace at the Alamo, "a home," as he put it. He did not want to leave. Other men at the Alamo agreed; on February 2 Jim Bowie sent Governor Smith this message: "Colonel Neill and myself have come to the solemn resolution that we will rather die in these ditches than give it up to the enemy."

Encouraging them somewhat was the arrival on February 3 of thirty men commanded by Colonel William Barret Travis, a twenty-six year old firebrand lawyer from Anahuac. Egotistical, proud, vain, with strong feelings about his own destiny, about glory and personal mission (three years previously he had written an autobiography), he was trouble in every sense of the word. He was highly critical, at times even contemptuous of authority, unless he was in command. For instance, at Anahuac in May, 1832, after the Mexican commander, Colonel John Bradburn, tried to curb smuggling with high-handed methods, blatantly infringing on personal liberties, Travis was arrested, along with his friend Patrick Jack, for their protests and opposition. When hundreds of Texans marched on the jail demanding the release of the two men, they found the two prisoners spread-eagled on the ground and Bradburn threatening to kill them unless the crowd dispersed immediately. "It was a moment made for Travis,"

Plan of the city of San Antonio and the Alamo drawn in 1836 by Colonel Ygnacio de Labastida for Santa Anna. Courtesy Barker Texas History Center, University of Texas, Austin.

historian Walter Lord observed. "Dramatically he called on his friends to fire; he would rather die a thousand deaths than permit this oppressor to remain unpunished." Again in June, 1835, he raised a company of twenty-five men to oppose Captain Antonio Tenorio, the Mexican commander at Anahuac, whom General Cós had instructed to prevent smuggling as well as uphold national authority. With unbelievable bravado Travis captured Tenorio and his soldiers without firing a shot, by brazenly ordering them to surrender or be put to the sword.

To many contemporaries (and historians as well) Travis was a paradox. He supported religion vigorously—and at times appeared to be quite "religious"—but he broke any number of the commandments. He was courteous and kind to women; yet he thought of them as sex objects, egotistically numbering his conquests in a well-detailed diary. At a first meeting or encounter he made an impressive figure. Six feet tall, 175 pounds, sinewy and rawboned, a nice-looking man with fair complexion, blue-gray eyes, and auburn hair which was almost curly, Travis could not—and did not—maintain a low profile. In the rustic frontier communities of Anahuac and San Felipe de Austin he was a fashion plate, "a dandy," sporting expensive boots and red pantaloons, shirts made from carefully selected materials, gloves, and a white hat. Yet he did not wear well with his colleagues. A man so ambitious, so determined to achieve greatness could never be popular, especially in frontier Texas where the idea of democracy, with every man an equal, ran contrary to Travis's emotional make-up. Unlike Jim Bowie, therefore, he never attracted men to him. They might admire his courage, respect his brainpower, be awed by his tenacity, but the love affair with himself excluded most, if not all, from his inner circle.

But make no mistake about Travis. Despite certain frailties, despite his egotism, he was a soldier—in spirit if not by profession—who held duty and honor more precious than life itself. Even though pleading with Governor Smith for an assignment other than the Alamo because, with Bowie and

W.B. Travis
By Wiley Martin
Dec. 1835

Courtesy Daughters of the Republic of Texas Library, San Antonio

Neill "already in charge," he would be "a subaltern," he would follow orders no matter how distasteful to his personal wants, no matter what the sacrifice. And if, perchance, anyone challenged his authority or tried to prevent him from carrying out an assignment, he became a formidable opponent, an implacable foe.

Even as Travis and his men were settling in at San Antonio, the Alamo garrison had another reason for rejoicing and renewed hope. On February 8 Colonel Davy Crockett, unannounced and unexpected, rode into town with twelve men who called themselves the Tennessee Company of Mounted Volunteers. Approaching the fifty-year mark, Crockett had already achieved a legendary status. During the previous three years three books had described—and often exaggerated —his abilities. After all, not many men could claim that they had ridden alligators for exercise, had shot six bucks in one day and forty-seven bears in a month, and had forced a ferocious grizzly to retreat merely by grinning at it.

Nor could they have better personfiied the American frontier. Born of parents who were always on the move and constantly "heels over head in debt," Crockett received very little formal education (six months to be exact). Yet by sheer force of will and dogged determination he fashioned a record of success. In the War of 1812 he fought with Andrew Jackson against the Creek Indians and afterwards against the Seminoles in Florida where he achieved the reputation of a fearless and intrepid soldier. Then he pioneered farms in Tennessee, repeatedly moving westward onto lands untouched by civiliza-tion. Not too surprisingly he soon became a recognized leaders as the ratio between man and nature increased—first as a magistrate, then as a state legislator, and in 1827 as a congressman from the Western District of Tennessee.

Crockett, however, did not have the intellectual and emotional capabilities for permanence. Although an articulate speaker with a flair for the dramatic, a marvelous raconteur of western folklore, and a wonderfully gregarious and outgoing personality, he lacked the depth of knowledge and the experience of history so necessary for survival in Washington. In other words, he had all of the right instincts but was unwilling to discipline himself, to maintain rigorous work habits, to punish himself for the sake of excellence. "When a man can grin and fight, flag a steamboat, or whip his weight in wildcats," he queried on more than one occasion, "what is the use of reading and writing?" As a consequence Crockett basked in the praise of those who would use him, oftentimes allowing them to help him formulate policy, to write his speeches, to a certain extent do his thinking. He soon found himself in conflict with President Andrew Jackson, whom he had supported upon first coming to Congress, and became associated with the opposition Whig Party. Having placed himself in opposition to the President, whom he called "a greater tyrant than Cromwell, Caesar or Bonaparte," Crockett found himself the object of attack. And in his reelection campaign of 1835, despite his warning that, if defeated, he would go to Texas and his constituents could go to hell, he was defeated by the Jackson forces by a slim majority of 230 votes.

So Crockett, true to his word and following an old precept "Be sure you are right, then go ahead," delivered his "Go to Hell" speech and disassociated himself from an impressive past. This decision, although seemingly precipitant and rash, was a very natural one for Crockett to make: the Mexican province of Texas was a "natural stompin' ground" for him. At last he would be with people who appreciated him and free from those scheming sophisticates in Washington. Once again he could be his fun-loving, exaggerative self, grabbing the spotlight and fascinating an audience. How well Crockett knew this role! Discarding his political garb, he dressed for the frontier, becoming a veritable advertisement for furs and animal pelts—a coonskin cap, a buckskin jacket and breeches, horn buttons, moccasins, and furs about the shoulders for warmth. Omnipresent in the crook of his arm was "Betsey," his famous rifle, which symbolized his hunting skills and prowess in the wilderness. And always within reach was another kind of weapon, a fiddle with which he charmed rather than threatened possible adversaries.

As Crockett proceeded to Texas, the anguish of rejection and the sting of defeat gradually faded—and noticeably his spirits began to revive. That this transformation occurred may have had something to do with the excitement of a new adventure and his release from societal restraints. Or possibly it revolved around the tenor of the times, around people rushing to a raw new land in behalf of liberty, around men once again fighting the age-old battle against tyranny and oppression. But whatever the reason the change took place. On January 9, 1836, upon reaching San Augustine, Texas, Crockett wrote his children that he had "taken the oath of government" and had "enrolled . . . as a volunteer for six months." Then he concluded: "I had rather be in my present situation than be elected to a seat in Congress for life." And soon after arrival at San Antonio, he became even more resolute in his convictions, announcing his determination to do whatever was necessary to defend "the liberties of our common country."

The command at the Alamo gradually began to take shape. On February 11 Colonel Neill, whom Walter Lord characterized as "a good second-rater," took a twenty-day leave of absence; the excuses, although somewhat obscure, suggested family illness and monetary obligations. But whatever the reasons, he created a problem by placing the twenty-six-year-old Travis in charge instead of the popular, steel-eyed Bowie. For three days the two men vied openly for power. Never one to "play second fiddle" to any man, Bowie rallied the men to his cause, plying them with several rounds of drinks before leading them around the Main Plaza to demand the release of all political prisoners being held in the city jail. Then when Travis called for an immediate election to choose a commander of the Alamo volunteers, Bowie won easily—and thus the two men were still face to face. The issue was soon resolved, however. Bowie, who late in January had "felt dreadfully sick," was once more afflicted, and this time "worse than ever." Although not fond of Travis, he realized that his own failing physical condition was hindering his ability to lead and, therefore, to defend. And he did endorse Travis's statement to Governor Smith on February 13 that the Alamo was "more important to occupy . . . than I first imagined. It is the key of Texas." Consequently the two men resolved their differences on February 14 in a surprisingly easy manner, especially after the furor of the past several days. They would retain their separate commands but would act jointly on all important decisions.

How quickly now the Alamo took on the character of a fort. With tensions between the commanders eliminated and distractions cast aside, the men worked feverishly and with renewed determination. Green Jameson, a lawyer from Kentucky, proved to be a highly imaginative engineer, building platforms of earth and timber to serve as parapets and gun mounts. He also reconstructed and fortified the palisade from the southeastern corner of the mssion to the Alamo chapel into a formidable defense barrier. Because of such help Captain Almeron Dickinson, a blacksmith from Gonzales who had a "knack for handling artillery," had almost completed his own particular assignment; he had placed all but three of the twenty cannon in key positions. At the same time Sam Blair, the ordnance head who was responsible for all ammunition, supplemented the small number of cannon balls by chopping up iron horseshoes for use as shrapnel. And while Hiram Williamson of Philadelphia, a former West Pointer, was drilling unwilling recruits who had no specific tasks and commissary chief John Baugh of Virginia was collecting forty-two cattle and a hundred bushels of corn, Dr. Amos Pollard of New York prepared the second floor of the long barracks as a hospital. Surprisingly he discovered that all necessary medical instruments except catheters and syringes were available.

Meanwhile, 365 miles south of the Alamo, preparations were taking place, the *Tamaulipas Gazette* announced, "to wipe out the stain in the blood of those perfidious foreigners would conquer Mexico's enemies; he was indeed, as he had designated himself, the "Napoleon of the West."

But Santa Anna was more than vanity and intrigue and opportunism. At times both imaginative and resourceful, he had registered successes through hard work and attention to detail. At Saltillo in January, 1836, where he was assembling his assault force for the Texas expedition, nothing escaped his scrutiny except teaching his soldiers the technique of shooting accurately. Having armed them with cumbersome, antiquated rifles which had tremendous recoil, he could not persuade his men to fire from the shoulder or to use the gun sight. He supervised everything else, however. Having already scraped together adequate funds to finance this campaign—from the church, from loan sharks, even using his own personal credit—he now applied his energies to bringing order out of chaos, to creating an army out of a mob. To General Vicente Filisola, his second-in-command, he issued orders in a rapid, staccato manner: acquire 100,000 pounds of hardtack, buy 500 horses for the cavalry, secure two-wheel and four-wheel carts as well as a comparable number of draft animals, mainly mules and oxen, for transporting supplies and baggage, attend to this and that detail. To General Eugenio Tolsa and Antonio Gaona, he was equally officious, demanding that they mold into a fighting force some 4,000 recruits, many of whom were Mayan Indians—the Yucatán battalion—"frightened, shivering men who did not understand the language" but who, upon pain of death, would obey orders instantly and without question. Then by mixing them with several "crack" brigades and swift, experienced cavalry units commanded by General Juan José Andrade, he was forming an army which was capable, he believed of annihilating all "traitors of Mexico" and restoring order to Texas.

By January 25, 1836, Santa Anna ordered his army, after a Grand Review of the troops, to move northward to the Rio Grande and San Antonio. How impressive the men looked, the officers in dark blue uniforms with scarlet fronts, the cavalry on spirited horses with sabres and lances glittering in the sun, and endless columns of infantrymen, almost 4,000 strong, in blue cotton uniforms and homemade sandals with tall black military hats complete with visor and plume on their heads. By the time they reached Monclova early in February, the march had become increasingly difficult and tortuous, at times even lethal. In the desert country of Coahuila the dust was choking, the terrain debilitating, each step of the way was draining the men of their energy and strength. Then, after passing through the old Spanish town of Presidio de Río Grande and crossing into Texas (only 119 miles from San Antonio), they suffered even greater hardships, even though reinforced by an additional 1,500 troops under General Ramírez y Sesma. The next day a Texas norther, with penetrating cold and chilling winds, kicking up sand and dust, brought a deluge of icy rain and glistening snow down upon them. So devastating were conditions that during a two-day period 100 oxen in Gaona's brigade died, Andrade's cavalrymen lost their way in a mesquite thicket, and the cotton-clad infantrymen, many without tents and camp equipage, huddled together, vainly trying to keep warm. The Mayan Indians, accustomed to a tropical clime, were especially vulnerable, with many succumbing to the bitter cold. Yet when a warming trend suddenly developed, so typical of South Texas weather, the army fared no better because a dry winter had depleted the natural forage, and water was scarce or nonexistent. As a result many animals "dropped with *mal de lengua,* a swelling of the tongue from thirst and dry fodder . . . others died of *telele,* a fever caused by stagnant water." As for the troops, conditions continued to worsen. Sorefooted to the point of exhaustion, weakened by an inadequate diet (Santa Anna was forced to cut the rations of hardtack in half), and blistered by an unforgiving sun, some of the men contracted diarrhea and dysentery; others fell exhausted along the way, waiting to die or be picked up by General Pedro Ampudio's artillerymen; and a few, who had enough stamina, tried to desert, excusing themselves because of the conditions or poor medical service or lack of pay; while most pushed doggedly forward, determined to complete this final segment of the march. At last on February 21 they arrived at the Medina River, only twenty-five miles from their objective. Now, with one swift thrust, Andrade and his cavalrymen could easily reach San Antonio in a day.

Although informed on February 18 by Blaz Herrera, a nephew of the highly respected Captain Juan Seguín, that a large Mexican force had crossed the Rio Grande and was advancing on San Antonio, Travis and Bowie were incredulous of all reports, discounting such stories as wild rumors, as "more Mexican lies." They could not believe that Santa Anna would attack before March 15. The wintry Texas weather of rain and ice would turn the rivers into raging torrents and the roads into a horrible mixture of mud and slush. Such conditions would make forced marches extremely difficult and the transporting of siege equipment almost impossible. Santa Anna would do the sensible thing.

But by early morning on February 23 Travis and Bowie could no longer discount such rumors. The Mexican population in San Antonio was astir. At a fandango on Soledad Street the previous night they had heard that a cousin of Mrs. Ambrosio Rodríguez named Rivas had seen Santa Anna in disguise— obviously reconnoitering the Texans' strength. As a result, an exodus was in full swing, families moving out of the city, their carts piled high with kitchen utensils and household goods, their faces registering stark, uncontrollable fear. By 11 A.M. the hubbub and commotion had increased to such an extent throughout the city that Travis tried to temper the panic by issuing orders that no one was to leave. Then a new rumor swept through the streets—the Mexican cavalry had reached Leon Creek, only eight miles away.

Travis acted quickly to calm this new anxiety. Together with Dr. John Sutherland of Alabama, he scurried to the highest point overlooking San Antonio, the old bell tower of San Fernando Church, where a sentry was on duty. To the south and west all three men anxiously scanned the horizon, but nothing disrupted their view, the arid, rather brownish countryside of mesquite and cactus and winter grass extending interminably, somewhat lazily before them. Yet to satisfy all doubts completely, Travis asked Sutherland and John W. Smith, who had distinguished himself in the storming of San Antonio in December, to reconnoiter the area, to make sure that no camouflaged Mexican army was lying in wait to surprise them.

By 1:30 that afternoon the two scouts had ridden approximately a mile and a half out of town when, upon crossing the crest of a hill, they came into full view of Andrade's cavalry in battle formation, estimated by Sutherland to be 1,500 strong. Frantically wheeling their horses about, they rode for the Alamo, while the sentry at San Fernando Church, watching their every move, sounded the alarm by ringing the tower bell. Now the terrifying rumors were a reality; now the scene in the city was bedlam, each clang of the old iron gong accentuating the dire circumstances of the moment. Taking no time to grab personal effects, Almeron Dickinson collected his wife Susannah and small child Angelina, then galloped on one horse to the Alamo. Bowie was at first concerned for his two sisters-in-law at the Veramendi home, but after securing them safely behind the Alamo walls, he hurriedly led a squad of volunteers to ransack huts and residences for grain or other provisions. Another group, by chance, happened upon thirty cattle and quickly herded them into the mission corral on the east side next to the "long barracks"; while others in their haste seized any equipment or possessions at hand, then pushed through the crowded streets to the fortress as the Mexican populace watched with wonderment at those who were about to "be killed."

Meanwhile inside the Alamo Travis worked feverishly in his headquarters room next to the west wall, using every precious minute before the enemy arrived. To Colonel James Fannin at Goliad (ninety-five miles distant) he sent a courier named Johnson with a note, pleading with him to bring his 450-man army to their aid immediately. To Davy Crockett who had just arrived and who impatiently blurted out, "Here

character, to come to our aid, with all dispatch—The enemy is receiving reinforcements daily & will no doubt increase to three or four thousand in four or five days. If this call is neglected, I am determined to sustain myself as long as possible & die like a soldier who never forgets what is due to his own honor & that of his country—
VICTORY OR DEATH.

William Barret Travis,
Lt. Col. Comdt.

Then as an afterthought he added:

P.S. The Lord is on our side—When the enemy appeared in sight we had not three bushels of corn—We have since found in deserted houses 80 or 90 bushels and got into the walls 20 or 30 heads of Beeves.

Travis

For the next four days the Texans were under continual bombardment; yet they sustained no casualties. Consequently, in spite of many discomforts—tasteless food and acrid substitutes for coffee, sleepless nights, and the bitter cold of a Texas norther (February 25) from which the men suffered at their posts on the walls—morale was high. But for how long Travis could not be sure. Every day more Mexican troops were arriving, thereby making the defense of the Alamo more and more difficult. Every day Santa Anna was drawing the circle tighter around them, piling up earthworks for new batteries just across the San Antonio River, occupying the makeshift buildings and crude huts of the area known as La Villita (little village) which was almost in the shadow of the Alamo, and ordering occasional probing attacks to test the fortress's defenses. Every day the battle drained the Texans mentally and physically, with Santa Anna waging a kind of psychological warfare by periodic bugle calls at night or short bursts of heavy cannonading to keep the defenders awake, as his men inched ever nearer to the walls. And always in sight from the tower of San Fernando Church was the blood-red flag, a constant reminder of the enemy's intentions.

On February 26 the Texans no longer returned the Mexican fire, now having to conserve their dwindling supply of ammunition. Because of the increasing seriousness of their predicament Travis thus sought every means to secure aid and reinforcements. That night he sent Captain Juan Seguín with a letter to Houston, hoping that his personal plea would have the desired effect:

> Do hasten on aid to me as rapidly as possible, as from the superior number of the enemy, it will be impossible for us to keep them out much longer. If they overpower us, we fall a sacrifice at the shrine of our country, and we hope posterity and our country will do our memory justice. Give me help, oh my country!

Again on February 27 Travis asked Jim Bonham to locate Colonel Fannin, then to plead with him for immediate assistance. His old friend was indeed ideal for this mission—a fine horseman, an expert swordsman, a persuasive speaker. But equally important, he knew the way to Goliad. Travis's message was direct enough. Fannin and his men could reach the Alamo without too much difficulty; they must come at once; otherwise they were dooming their compatriots to a choice between surrender and death.

Within the last twenty-four hours, however, Santa Anna had tired of seeing a steady stream of messengers entering and leaving the beleaguered fort and had taken corrective measures to remedy this ridiculous situation. At least such activity hereafter would be extremely hazardous. Yet at departure time Bonham was resolute in his determination and confident in his ability. He vowed to elude all enemy roadblocks, consult with Fannin, and, God willing, return within a few days. And what would be his reentrance signal into the Alamo, his identification to the sentries on the walls? He would tie a white handkerchief around his hat. Then as he spurred his horse into the black emptiness of the night, Travis assured him: "I'll have the men watching from the walls. We'll see you and be ready at the gates."

So now the waiting began, either for the hoped for relief force or a final assault by the Mexican army. To relieve the monotony and tension of these days, the tedium of long hours at being stationed on the walls, the suffering caused by limited provisions and inclement weather (another norther struck on February 29), the men of the Alamo effectively countered Santa Anna's tactics of psychological warfare with their own unique methods. On at least two occasions they ventured outside the walls on limited sorties, one to test Sesma's troops who were threatening them with cannonading, and the other to set afire and destroy the structures protecting Mexican soldiers at nearly La Villita. Bowie, desperately ill and growing feebler, also tried to bolster morale by having his cot carried into the mission compound where he encouraged the men to persevere and endure. But Crockett, at his innovative, daring, exaggerative best, proved to be the perfect medicine for the men during those long hours. At his command post between the southeast corner and the chapel he would stand or kneel atop the palisade, "rest his long gun and fire"—and he "rarely missed his mark." Then "seemingly indifferent to the shots fired at him" and unconcerned for his own personal safety, he "railed at" the enemy, ridiculing their manhood as well as their marksmanship. And when off duty he devised an entertaining diversion for his comrades, a "musical duel" in noise making, featuring John McGregor and his bagpipes versus Davy Crockett and his fiddle.

But no amount of distraction or psychology could alter cold, hard facts. No matter that reinforcements from Gonzales arrived on March 1, a company of thirty-two men led by George Kimball and Albert Martin, no matter that Travis was encouraged that other groups might also swell their ranks, the men of the Alamo were outnumbered fifteen or twenty to one. The Mexican army numbered at least 3,000 men, then 1,000 more with accommpanying cannon on March 3. Increasingly now Santa Anna upped the activity of his army—and the circle became smaller and ever tighter. Only 400 yards on the west was Sesma with his howitzers, continually lobbing cannonballs into every part of the compound or pounding the walls and earthworks; approximately 300 yards to the south was La Villita, a den of enemy activity and commotion; 1,000 yards on the southeast was a powderhouse, 800 yards on the northeast a wide, protective ditch, and 800 yards on the north an old mill, all serving as the nearest jumping off points for an attack. Then during the early morning hours of March 4 the Mexicans moved guns into place on the north, less than 250 yards away, and began firing point-blank at the walls, seemingly attempting to batter the fortress into rubble. In plain sight also were Mexican work details, obviously preparing scaling ladders and other equipment vital to an all-out assault. And always omnipresent, fluttering from the tower of San Fernando Church, was the blood-red flag.

Actually on March 3 the Texans realized their fate. Bonham, after racing to Goliad and vainly pleading with Fannin for immediate relief, returned to San Antonio with a discouraging reply. From one of the nearby heights overlooking the fortress, as he surveyed Travis's hopeless position, a fellow courier tried to dissuade him from rejoining his comrades, from throwing his life away. But Bonham replied in much the same way as he had to Fannin who begged him to remain at Goliad: "I will report the result of my mission to Travis, or die in the attempt." And report he did. With a white handkerchief attached to his hat and flapping in the breeze, he galloped past the startled Mexicans. The Alamo gates at the south wall opened, and he was in.

Yet despite Bonham's disheartening report the men of the Alamo continued to fight. In a final letter to the "President of the Convention" which was meeting at Washington-on-the-Brazos to decide the matter of Texas independence, Travis recorded their sense of duty, their determination to defend the Alamo, their resignation to death rather than surrender. In part, he wrote:

> I look to the colonies alone for aid: unless it arrives soon, I shall have to fight the enemy on his own terms. I will, however, do the best I can under the circumstances; and I am confident that the determined valor, and the desperate courage, heretofore evinced by my men will not fail them in the last struggle: and although they may be sacrificed to the vengeance of a gothic enemy, the victory will cost the enemy so dear, that it will be worse for him than defeat . . . God and Texas— Victory or Death!

For three more days the Alamo withstood heavy cannonading and attack, the men awaiting the moment of final assault. Actually some of the Anglo and Mexican "rebels" could have saved themselves, it being a rather simple matter to slip past enemy sentries under the cover of darkness; however, only one man, named Louis Rose, chose to do so. But the story of Travis standing before his command in the mission compound and asking those who would die with him to step across a line which he drew in the ground with a sword—and Bowie, on a cot, commanding his men to carry him across the line—has proven to be legendary. Yet, these men never needed a build-up, for they left all Texans and Americans a glorious heritage; they were ready to die for their compatriots and fight for liberty rather than save themselves.

Early in the morning of March 6 the defenders of the Alamo

Louis Eyth, *The Speech of Travis to His Men at the Alamo.* Courtesy Daughters of the Republic of Texas Library, San Antonio.

spent their last hours in violent conflict. At a little past 5 A.M. Santa Anna ordered a frontal assault from four separate columns, using many of the newly trained Indian recruits as cannon fodder. After braving heavy cannonading of ball and grape as well as deadly rifle fire (each Texan had as many as four or five loaded weapons at his side), the Mexican soldiers fell back, regrouped, and moved forward a second time, only to be driven back again. Finally on the third attempt they were able to reach the Alamo, a mass of terrified humanity collecting under the north wall, since the Mexican columns from both the east and west had veered in that direction because of the deadly fire by the defenders. Yet, since few of the men had scaling ladders, they were stymied for the moment.

Santa Anna, however, realized that victory was in his grasp. So he quickly called forth those reserves who were his most experienced soldiers. Running at full speed toward the Alamo, cheering wildly and firing intermittently, they reached the walls with relatively few casualties, but found themselves in much the same predicament as the troops under the north wall—no scaling ladders. Then General Juan V. Amador and a small contingent surged forward, clawing and grasping at the walls, using their comrades' bodies as rungs and stepping stones, and dropped inside the mission compound. Their orders were clear and explicit; above the din of battle there arose the music from the Mexican military bands playing the thrilling, blood-curdling strains of the *Duguello*, "the traditional Spanish march of no quarter . . . of throat-cutting and merciless death."

For fifteen minutes the struggle continued. Because of the fury of the battle, accounts have differed on what happened. No one knows, therefore, how the men of the Alamo specifically died. Travis most likely was killed on the north wall in the first assault, a bullet hitting him in the head. His last words were typical of the man. Encouraging several of Captain Juan Seguín's men, he yelled out in Spanish: "No rendirse, muchachos"—"Don't surrender, boys." Crockett may have fallen at the southeast palisade with his Tennessee

Henry Arthur McArdle's seven-by-twelve-foot painting, *Dawn at the Alamo*, was completed in 1883 after seven years of work. Courtesy Archives Division, Texas State Library.

Louis Eyth, *Death of Bowie: A Command from the Mexicans that He Be Killed.* Courtesy Daughters of the Republic of

The Fall of the Alamo by Robert J. Onderdonk, 1903. Oil on canvas, 5x7 ft. *Courtesy Friends of the Governor's Mansion, Austin.*

boys, taking a heavy toll of enemy soldiers before being dealt "a deadly blow" with a sword and then "pierced by not less than 20 bayonets." In the Enrique de la Peña *Diary*, however, it was recorded that he surrendered along with five other men and was summarily executed by Santa Anna. Bowie was either already dead from fever or was quickly killed on his cot in one of the mission rooms, and Dickinson died atop the chapel while firing a cannon. Most probably Bonham, who had returned from Goliad on March 3, although knowing that the situation was hopeless, also fell next to Dickinson. But one report had him battling his way toward the powder magazines when cut down, intent upon blowing up as many of the enemy as possible. Surely such action was symbolic of the fighting during those last desperate minutes.

Later that morning Santa Anna, while looking over the carnage that had taken place inside the Alamo, remarked to one of his officers that "it was but a small affair." But he was wrong. While 183 Texas "rebels" died that day, his attacking army probably lost 600 men killed and wounded—or approximately one-third of the assault force. More important, however, were the effects of those thirteen days at the Alamo. After hearing of the heroic stand at the Alamo by Travis and his men and after learning that Santa Anna had unceremoniously stacked and burned their bodies, the Texas leaders realized that they must put aside personal jealousies and petty quarrels for the common good. True! the men of the Alamo had perished but, as one historian put it, "their spirits had only begun to live and inspire."